Giants
Angus McAskill
and Anna Swan

Jacqueline Langille

Four East Publications Ltd.
P.O. Box 29
Tantallon, Nova Scotia B0J 3J0

Copyright 1990
All rights reserved

1st printing November 1990

edited by Hilary Sircom
design by Paul McCormick
printing and typesetting by
    McCurdy Printing & Typesetting Limited
    Halifax, Nova Scotia, Canada

Acknowledgements

The publisher wishes to express his appreciation for the generous financial support of the **Nova Scotia Department of Tourism and Culture** and the **Canada Council.**

The publisher and author acknowledge the following people and organizations for their help in the preparation of this book: Mrs. Ethel Francis and Mr. George Swan, both of North Sydney, N.S.; Mermaid Theatre of Nova Scotia, Windsor; and The Giant Angus McAskill Heirs Society, Englishtown, Cape Breton.
The publisher and author are indebted to Margaret Campbell, Photograph Archivist at the Public Archives of Nova Scotia, Halifax, for her invaluable help in the location of visuals for this book.

Richard Rogers, Publisher

Canadian Cataloguing in Publication Data
Langille, Jacqueline, 1966-

    Angus McAskill and Anna Swan

    (Famous Maritimers)
    Bibliography: p.
    ISBN 0-920427-20-0

1. Swan, Anna, 1846-1888. 2. McAskill, Angus, 1825-1863. 3. Giants — Nova Scotia — Biography. I. Title. II. Series.

GN69.2.L36 1989   573'.8'0922   C89-098598-7

Preface

There is for all of us a fascination in discovering how people lived in the past. Most adults are familiar with the questions, "What was it like when you were growing up?" and "What did you do when you were my age?" The series is intended to address this interest and to make available to young people some of the material previously found only in books directed towards the adult market. Although the biographies have been kept brief, the bibliographies will suggest reading for those who would like to do further research.

These Famous Maritimers who were pioneers and innovators in their day are our local heroes and heroines; the contribution they made to our way of life is recorded in our museums and historic homes. We hope that this series will increase awareness of our Maritime heritage both for those who already live here and for the visitors who may wish to stay awhile in order to get to know us and our history better.

Hilary Sircom
General Editor

Contents

Giant McAskill's clothes, boot, cane and chair at Englishtown, Cape Breton.

Courtesy of Public Archives of Nova Scotia.

Introducing the Giants: Angus McAskill 1825-63 Anna Swan 1846-88

Sometimes a person is a hero because of what he has to say or the deeds he performs, such as Robin Hood or Louis Riel. Sometimes people are heroes just because of who they are, for example members of the Royal Family or film stars.

Folk heroes are usually people who seem to be larger than life and who have been looked up to because they achieved fame in their often simple surroundings. Two of Nova Scotia's folk heroes were indeed larger than life. They were giants whose lifetimes overlapped in the nineteenth century and who became famous not only for their size, both being well over seven feet ten, but also for their kind natures, gentle hearts and the good examples they set.

We now know that giantism is caused by a malfunction of the pituitary gland which is located at the base of the brain and produces the growth hormone. As a person reaches the teenage years, normally a second

5

hormone is produced which slows down growth. If the system is not working properly then the growth hormone keeps on working and people grow into giants. On the other hand there are people who lack the growth hormone and they may remain small, as dwarfs.

Sometimes we see people in professional sports, who are as tall as seven feet but in North America today the average height of a man is five feet ten inches and of a woman five feet four inches. In the 1800's, giants were very rare and most people had never heard of, and certainly had never seen one, so our two heroes caused a sensation wherever they went.

Passengers aboard an emigration vessel.

Angus McAskill's Early Life

Off the west coast of Scotland are a group of islands called the Hebrides. Here, on the tiny island of Bernerary, Norman and Christina McAskill earned a living by farming and fishing. Their son, Angus, was born in 1825.

Norman was in his forties, and Christina in her thirties when they decided to move their family to the New World. Many Scottish people left their homes at this time, hoping they would be more successful as farmers and fishermen in North America. Many moved to Cape Breton because its landscape reminded them so much of their native Scotland. Angus McAskill was six years old when his father purchased some farm land in Cape Breton, and the family set sail across the Atlantic Ocean to start a new life.

They landed at a place called St. Ann's, on St. Ann's Bay, Victoria County, Cape Breton Island. The area was called "Englishtown," because the original settler had not spoken Gaelic, which was the normal language of the Scottish people. The land was covered with thick forests and Angus' father had to build a house for his family and plant oats and potatoes so they would have food for their first winter.

McAskill soon had his farm growing well and found the bay teeming with fish, so his family did not go hungry. Angus grew up learning how to farm and fish just like his father and was sent, with the other children, to study at the one-room school run by Alexander Munro. There were thirteen children in the McAskill family and their father could afford to pay for only a few terms of study for each one. Thirty-seven students, ranging in age from five to seventeen, attended this school, many of them boarding with Mr. Munro because the journey to the school was long and hard in the winter.

At this time Angus was no bigger than the other boys; in fact he was rather a small child and, although his father was five feet nine inches, no one ever expected him to grow so much. Then as he turned twelve he started to shoot up, soon overtaking the friends with whom he played and wrestled. He had never liked fighting, for he was a good-natured boy, but a good wrestle for fun was all right. It was all right for the other boys, too, until Angus started winning all the time!

By the age of fourteen, Angus McAskill became known as *Gille Mhor*, which is Gaelic for Big Boy. He was now very tall and appeared to be slow and clumsy. He was slow because he was not used to his large size, and he was clumsy because the world he lived in was not built for extra-large people. He just did not fit very well. Some people said it was the marvellous climate of Cape Breton which had caused Angus to grow so tall; others said maybe it was the bowl of oatmeal and cream called *crowdie*, which he ate after every meal from the age of eight until maturity. Still other people pointed to the giants of Scotland's past, and said Angus had inherited his enormous size from them.

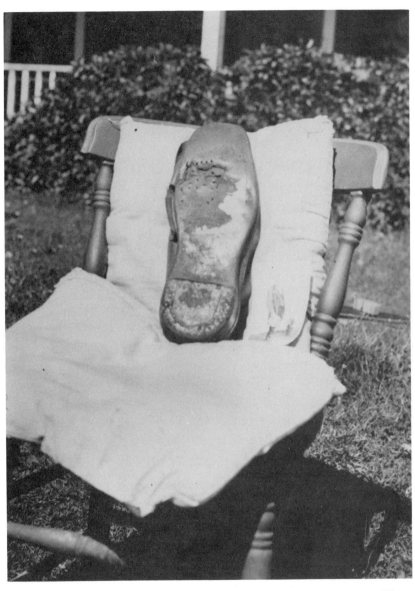

Giant McAskill's shoe at Bay View Hotel, Why-cocomagh.

Interior of a Scottish peasant's cottage.

Courtesy of Public Archives of Canada.

Whatever made him so big, his father soon realized that his son needed more room. He altered the house so the ceilings on both levels were raised enough to give Angus head room. His father also built him an eight-foot long bed which was sprung with ropes to support the mattress and his massive weight. Although Norman fixed the ceilings for his son, he was never able to change the door into the house, so Angus always had to bend down when he came in.

Angus was different from everyone else in the community and sometimes, as he was growing up, he was teased.

With advice and help from his father and the local minister, he learned how to handle the rudeness of others. Like all the other Scottish families in the area the McAskill family was deeply religious. Angus went to church, read the Bible, and learned to control his temper.

That Angus learned to endure teasing the hard way is shown by the following story. Once he had gone with the crew of a fishing boat to North Sydney. In the evening they all went ashore to a community dance called a *ceilidh* (pronounced cay-lee). Angus was not wearing shoes, so he did not join the dance but sat at the side enjoying the music. One young man could not resist stepping on Angus' bare toes as he danced by. Angus was angry but, knowing it would be wrong to start a fight, ignored the insult. Again the young man danced by and laughed as he again stomped on Angus' toes. A third time the dancer came by, but as the young man stepped forward, Angus could no longer contain himself; he jumped up and punched his tormenter right in the face! The young man flew into the middle of the floor and landed unconscious, being knocked out for so long that it was thought he might have died.

When the crew returned to their fishing boat, the captain found Angus by his bunk, on his knees praying that he had not killed a man. His prayer was answered as the young man recovered.

Angus McAskill as a young man.

Courtesy of Public Archives of Nova Scotia.

Angus as a Young Man: Stories Get Around

Not only was Angus growing very tall, he was also becoming one of the strongest men in Cape Breton. One day, his father and brothers were trying to lift a very heavy log up on to a special sawing rack. The rack was six feet in the air, and hung over a pit. One man would stand in the pit under the log and hold the end of the saw, while two other men would stand above and pull on the other end. Lunchtime came and still they could not lift the heavy log up onto the rack. During the meal, Angus' father scolded him for not giving them a hand so Angus quietly went out, and all by himself lifted the heavy log that three men had not been able to move. When his father saw this he did not believe Angus had done it alone and accused him of playing a trick. Angus became very upset that his father would not believe him and to prove his point knocked the log off the rack, then reached down and picked it up again. He apologized to his father for getting angry, while his father decided never again to doubt Angus' strength or his word.

Big Angus worked at all the hard and heavy chores of the farm, but he was best at plowing; he and his father made a perfect team. Once, a neighbour bet them ten dollars that the field they were then plowing could not be finished that afternoon. In those pioneer days, ten dollars was too great a sum to be turned down. In the middle of the field, one of the horses suddenly became lame, but, not to be defeated, Angus stepped into the harness beside the other horse and his father directed the plow. The lad pulled just as well as the large farm horse, and they would have won the bet if Angus' mother had not seen them and become upset at the sight of her son pulling the plow. They were obliged to stop and Angus had to pay out the ten dollars. However, he was content to keep his mother happy.

Even in his twenties Angus was still growing. When he reached his prime he was seven feet nine inches tall, weighing close to five hundred pounds, with feet eighteen inches long and hands twelve inches long. With his blue eyes and dark curly hair and his well-proportioned body, he was a pleasant-looking giant. His voice had a hollow musical tone and people enjoyed talking to him. Although he was so large he was not at all frightening but more of a "friendly giant".

Angus loved fishing in the bay and every morning, during the fishing season, when he was not too busy on the farm, he would be out at dawn in his own half-ton boat which had extra ballast (weights) before the mast to balance his weight in the stern. He earned enough by his fishing to support himself and help out his family.

The local fishermen still liked to tease Angus. They were all his friends, but sometimes could not resist a practical joke. Once when Angus asked for help to pull his boat up onto the shore above the high tide water mark, a group of fishermen decided to play a trick on him. He pulled on one side while the group of men pulled on the other. They secretly planned to pull his boat right over the shore, and into a swamp. As they passed the high water mark and Angus realized they were not going to stop, he dug in his heels and pulled back on the boat. The men kept on tugging and the boat was pulled apart! After that, the men of English-town were more careful in their teasing of the Giant Angus McAskill.

Tales of his size and strength were spreading around the countryside. People were amazed and began to

Beach at St. Ann's, Cape Breton.

Courtesy of Public Archives of Nova Scotia.

Angus' home at Englishtown, Cape Breton.

come and challenge him to wrestle in order to prove his strength. Angus felt that fighting was wrong and always tried to avoid it.

One day a famous fighter came to Cape Breton to challenge the giant. Angus treated the man kindly, made him feel at home but refused to fight. The man became angry and rude and this so annoyed Angus that he asked him to leave. At the door they shook hands to say good-bye and Angus squeezed so hard that the blood all went to the fighter's fingertips. He never again asked the giant to fight.

Another time the captain of an American fishing vessel, who had heard of Giant Angus while buying bait in St. Ann's, went to the McAskill farm to challenge Angus to fight. When Angus said he would not, the three-hundred-pound captain refused to leave. So, Angus simply picked him up and threw him over the wood-pile which was ten feet high and twelve feet wide. The captain left as fast as he could get himself up off the ground!

Giant Angus earned a reputation as a good and kindly neighbour who could be called upon for help in times of need. When crops failed, and the winters were long, Cape Bretoners had a hard time surviving. One poor farmer begged a merchant for some flour on credit to help out his family. The merchant had to refuse his plea but told him that he could have a whole barrel of flour from his ship down at the dock, if he could find some way to get it out of the hold. A barrel of flour was very heavy, and as the hold was at least twelve feet deep, the farmer did not have much hope until he thought of Giant McAskill. Angus went down to the boat and tossed four kegs of flour into the water beside the ship, fished them out and loaded them onto the farmer's wagon. All he needed was a "thank you" for his trouble.

Giant Angus goes on Tour

In 1849, when Angus was twenty-four, an American fishing captain, named Dunseith, offered to help him make his fortune by taking him on tour. Angus did not really want to go, neither did his family want to lose him, but the money sounded good in those hard times. Mr. Dunseith promised that Angus would become rich and live like a gentleman, so he sadly decided to leave the farm and try the life of show business.

"The Giant McAskill" was first exhibited in Halifax. People were eager to pay to see a man of such great size; he always toured as a giant, and never as a "strong man". After touring with Dunseith for a couple of years, Angus had his own manager, a Yarmouth man called Noah Fifield. His travels took him throughout Nova Scotia, Newfoundland and Québec and down into the United States. The crowds loved him because he was such a very open man who always answered any questions he was asked, never minded being stared at, and often performed exercises to show how well his gigantic body worked. Thousands paid to see him.

Before touring in the United States, Angus had never seen a train. One day, some robbers tried to hold up the train on which he was travelling. As they came into the car to rob the passengers, Giant Angus rose to his full height and with his broad forty-four inch wide

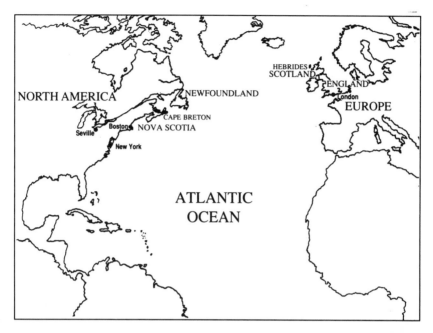

shoulders towered above them. The robbers turned and fled!

Angus' first visit home after a season of touring was quite an exciting affair for St. Ann's, for everyone wanted to see if the *Gille Mhor* had changed. He certainly had; no longer was he the clumsy shy "Big Boy" of the town. Wearing beautifully tailored expensive clothes, he walked proudly and spoke with confidence. He was becoming known all over the world and his old friends and neighbours were happy for him.

Angus' tours took him as far away as the West Indies and also to England where he was invited to Windsor Castle to meet Queen Victoria. They chatted informally for a while and the Queen was most impressed by the giant's astounding size and gentle

Giant McAskill with Parson Taylor.

manners. She presented him with gifts and complimented him warmly. Angus always felt very honoured to have met his Queen.

The only part of his life as a celebrity which Angus did not like was that he had little chance to see the towns he visited. His agent said that people would never pay a dollar to see a giant, if they could see him for nothing in the street. This made sense to Angus, especially since he was making good money, much of which he sent home to help out his family. However, once the first rush to see him was over, Angus could walk about the place he was visiting and, because he missed St. Ann's Bay, would make for the nearest water.

On his last tour, he was walking along a dock somewhere in the United States (some say New Orleans, others New York) when he came upon a huge anchor weighing over a ton. Sailors nearby who had heard tales of the giant's remarkable strength, challenged him to lift it. McAskill had never yet been defeated by any feat of strength, and he heaved that huge anchor and walked down the dock with it, to the amazement of the onlookers. However, when he went to set it down, somehow one of the flukes caught his shoulder and caused him so much pain that even the people watching had tears in their eyes.

Doctors in the mid-1800s had nothing like X-rays to help them discover what was wrong, so they could not do much for the Giant, and it was never known exactly how badly he had been hurt. Although he recovered after a while, he never really regained his health.

Retirement of a Giant

Giant McAskill now decided it was time to retire from this touring life and he came back to St. Ann's with a secure fortune, a wealthy man for those days. The Englishtown area he returned to was a different place in the 1850s because many of his former neighbours had followed their minister to settle land in New Zealand.

Angus was glad to be home. He used some of his money to help his relatives, friends and neighbours, then built a store and went into business supplying groceries and other goods. He had the store specially built with large living rooms above. The building had raised ceilings and nine-foot door frames. Here he would sit, on a 140-gallon molasses keg, talking to his customers and sometimes smoking his pipe which had been specially carved out of the trunk of a cherry tree, with one of the branches hollowed out for the stem.

The store was a success because Angus had a good mind for business. He treated everyone fairly and charged only the necessary price on the goods he sold. He did not like to give credit but was so kind that he would never refuse to help those in need. He sold tea by the pound, or by the fistful for the same price. One man demanded a pound hoping to get as much as possible for his money. Angus grabbed a fistful anyway, weighed it, and found it to be over a pound. The

Giant McAskill's cane and hat, Englishtown, Cape Breton.

customer was very surprised, but Angus gave him only the pound he had requested.

Also successful was the grist-mill which Angus bought on Munro's Point. Sometimes, if the stream which turned the mill wheel ran dry, the giant would push the mill stones by himself. He could carry the four-bushel bags of wheat and oats about the mill as easily as if they had been loaves of bread.

As the years went by, Giant Angus' health failed, maybe from delayed effects of the anchor accident, or perhaps from more pituitary gland problems (certainly his hands and feet had never stopped growing). He may have suffered also from rheumatism as his bones became worn out from carrying his huge weight. He no longer travelled far but his hospitality was well known and he welcomed visitors. He had never been a boastful man, but would gladly tell tales of adventure from his touring years. He remained deeply religious all his life but, when he returned to St. Ann's to live, he did not go to church because the congregation would spend the whole service staring at him.

His was a comfortable life, but it did not last long as, on August 1, 1863, Angus suddenly became very ill. The doctor diagnosed "brain fever," and he was taken to his parents' house and put to bed in his old bed which had to be lengthened again to fit him. Here, seven days later, he died with his mother and father and Reverend Abraham McIntosh at his bedside. He was only thirty-four years old.

Two local carpenters worked six hours to build his pine coffin which was reported to be eight feet long, two feet six inches wide and one foot three inches high, large enough to float three men across St. Ann's Bay. Angus McAskill was buried in the church graveyard overlooking the bay he had loved so much. A huge crowd gathered to say good-bye to their friend, neighbour and hero, Cape Breton's Giant, the big man with a big heart.

Memorial at grave site of Giant McAskill.

Courtesy of N.S.I.S.

Anna Swan's Childhood

In the year that Angus McAskill was celebrating his twenty-first birthday in St. Ann's, Cape Breton, about a hundred and fifty miles away as the crow flies, in Mill Brook near New Annan, Colchester County, Nova Scotia's famous giantess was born.

It seemed like a miracle when Mrs. Ann Swan gave birth to an eighteen-pound baby girl. Alexander Swan and the local country doctor could hardly believe their eyes; the third child of the Swan family was more than twice the size of a normal baby!

The Swan's new child had bright blue eyes and her parents named her Anna Haining Swan. They knew their Annie was different from the very beginning, as she grew so fast that her cradle and her clothes had to be replaced almost as soon as they were made. Her parents were of normal height, and they could never understand why Annie grew so much. By the age of four, she was four feet six inches, almost as tall as her mother, but still of course, at heart, a little girl who loved to sit on the floor and play with her dolls.

One day a stranger to the area, a travelling salesman, stopped at her parents' house. When he saw Annie playing on the kitchen floor, he thought she was much older and called her a "daftie". When he discovered that she was only four years old, he was very surprised and told Mr. Swan that people would

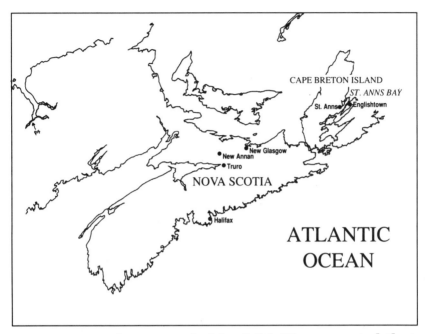

CAPE BRETON ISLAND
ST. ANNS BAY
St. Anns   Englishtown
New Glasgow
New Annan
Truro
NOVA SCOTIA
Halifax

ATLANTIC
OCEAN

pay to see such a remarkable child. He suggested that Mr. Swan should take Annie on tour, exhibiting her to the general public.

In March, 1851, Mr. Alexander Swan took his daughter to Halifax to exhibit her as the "Infant Giantess". He took her to the local fairs and many people came to see her. Everyone who saw Annie was amazed at the size of this beautiful child and there were articles about her in the Halifax newspapers. When she was on tour in Pictou, her mother stayed with her, because she was still very shy and people marvelled how the normal-sized woman could have had such an enormous child.

Annie was growing too big for her surroundings. At the age of six, she was taller than her five foot four inch father. Their home had not been built for large people, and she soon outgrew the dining table, so had to eat her meals while sitting on the floor with her back against a wall for support. Her father had to buy a special long bed to fit her. As she grew up, the doorways of the house caused her many health problems because she always had to stoop to go through them. Her mother had trouble making her extra-large clothing and finding a shoemaker to make her giant-sized shoes. Annie was uncomfortable with all the trouble her great size caused at home.

People in New Annan soon began to call Annie Swan "Big Ann". She had problems sometimes at school because other children teased her about her height. She had grown much too large for an ordinary desk, so she sat on a stool and worked on a table that was raised on planks as she kept growing. She did not like being different.

As she was not happy at school, Annie would rather stay home and help her mother and father with all the chores of running a farm and raising a family. (Her mother had ten more normal children in the years Annie was growing up.) Annie loved the country she lived in and one of the things she liked best was to take long walks in the open fields where no one could tease her; there, at least, she could stand tall and not worry about her height.

Annie reached seven feet when she was only fifteen years old. People who saw her for the first time would stop and ask questions. She was always being bothered and hated all this attention. Her parents were worried about her and sent her to live with an aunt in Truro hoping that a change would make their Big Ann feel better.

Anna in white dress next to a woman of normal size.

In Truro Annie attended the Normal School. She had always wanted to be a teacher so she studied hard and did very well. However, she was still unhappy. Crowds of people would follow her down the Truro streets just to say they had seen the giantess. Her aunt tried to be kind, but Annie was too big; she felt clumsy, and out of place, always bumping into things and breaking ornaments around the house.

Her parents were glad to have her back when Annie returned without even finishing the year of school, and the girl tried hard to be happy leading a quiet life at home.

Anna Swan standing between her parents.

Courtesy of G. Swan.

Anna Finds Her Own Place

In 1862, one of the Swan's neighbours from Pictou, a Quaker gentleman, was travelling in New York, U.S.A. He went to see Mr. Phineas T. Barnum who had a museum and show which exhibited strange animals and even stranger people. The Quaker told Mr. Barnum about his seven-and-a-half-foot neighbour. The showman was very interested, and asked to be sent the girl's exact height and measurements. When he received this information he sent his agent to Nova Scotia to offer Annie Swan a job.

Annie was too shy to think about show business and her parents twice refused Mr. Barnum's agent. They were afraid of the dangers of big cities in the States and did not want their daughter to go anywhere all by herself. The third time Mr. Barnum offered, his agent was a man named Judge H.P. Ingalls who made an offer the Swan family could not refuse. Annie was promised $1,000 a month to appear in P.T. Barnum's Museum on Broadway. The farm had not been doing well and Annie really wanted to help her family, so they all agreed she should accept this offer and her parents travelled with her to New York City.

When Annie met Mr. Barnum, she was sixteen and had reached her maximum height of seven feet eleven inches. P.T. Barnum had promised that "Big Ann" would be exhibited like a lady, and he had special living quarters made to measure for her. When she was settled, and finally comfortable in a world built for her, with a private teacher provided for three hours a day so she could continue her studies, her parents went back to Nova Scotia.

Annie had at last found a place where she could be happy. She had rooms just right for her size, beautiful clothes made of fine material, and money to help her family. She made friends with people who would never tease her, because they were just as different as she was, like the Living Skeleton, the Dog-faced Boy, Tom Thumb, and others. For all her shyness, surprisingly Annie did not mind being exhibited. The thousands of people who came to visit her while she worked for Mr. Barnum were amazed at her size and did not make fun of her.

Giants have always been much rarer than dwarves and, in Annie's time, several famous dwarves were touring the world. Barnum paired Annie with a dwarf called Commodore Nutt who weighed only twenty-four pounds and stood just twenty-nine inches tall. He looked like a doll next to the giantess and they became good friends. Barnum had hired several male giants, but Annie was the only known giantess at that time. While she worked with Barnum, a couple of giants tried to win her affection, but Annie was not interested in marrying yet.

The Giantess enjoyed meeting people and was always willing to talk to those who came to see her. She loved her new life, but was often thinking of her home in Nova Scotia. She sent much of her salary to her parents, and tried to go home for a visit every year. On one of her first visits home, people crowded around to see the famous giantess who was still their "Big Ann".

She drove up in a large carriage and stepped down without any help, whereas most women needed a wooden box step and a helping hand. One of the people

Anna Swan with her parents.

Courtesy of Public Archives of Nova Scotia.

she went to visit was surprised when the antique sofa Anna sat on tipped up like a seesaw with her great weight on one end!

On July 13, 1865, a fire broke out in the Barnum Museum and Anna was trapped on an upper floor. As she could not get out herself, and no one could carry her, a loft derrick, used for building large structures, was brought and Big Ann was hoisted on a tackle by eighteen men, lifted and lowered from the building. The crowd cheered her rescue. This fire destroyed all Anna's savings of $1,200 and her nerves were shattered. She returned to Nova Scotia to recover but found she missed her career and her friends. So the Nova Scotian Giantess went back to the United States again to work for Mr. Barnum at the new American Museum. Another fire, March 3, 1868, destroyed this museum also, and Mr. Barnum decided to retire from the exhibition business.

By October of that year, Big Ann was to be found touring Nova Scotia towns. At her shows, she would wrap a tape measure around her waist and then ask a woman in the audience to put the same tape round her own waist. The tape which went once around Anna would go three times around the average woman. Although she was so large, she did not look awkward or ungainly; in fact she was thought to be very beautiful and was admired for her modesty and grace.

After two years of touring, giving shows in church halls and at local fairs, Anna began to miss the excitement of show business in the United States. In 1879, she went back to New Jersey to join Judge H.P. Ingalls, who, as her manager, took Anna on tour all over the eastern United States.

Anna standing with couple of normal size looking at her.

Courtesy of G. Swan.

Anna Swan and her husband, Captain Martin Van Buren Bates, with a man of average height.

Courtesy of Public Archives of Nova Scotia.

Marriage of Two Giants

Giantess Anna had been a success ever since she had started touring. She had not married because she thought most of the men she met were only after her money and wanted to be a part of her success. Finally, at the home of General Winfield Scott at Mount Washington, New Jersey, Anna Swan met the man she had been waiting for all her life. Captain Martin Van Buren Bates was also a giant, standing seven feet nine inches tall. He was a real gentleman from the Southern States, and as he had been touring for several years had his own income. When they met, they felt made for each other.

Anna's career kept them apart for a while, but on April 22, 1871, they both set sail for Europe on the same tour with the Ingalls' group of performers. The cruise to Europe was just long enough for Anna and Captain Bates to become very good friends and before the ship reached Europe, they had announced their engagement. Everyone was delighted for the two giants.

On June 2, 1871, the couple was invited to meet Queen Victoria. She was most impressed, as she had been years earlier by Giant Angus McAskill, with their size and the elegance of their manners. The Queen was also very happy that they were to be married and presented them with wedding gifts including a diamond ring. She had a satin dress made for Anna to

Anna's wedding in London, England 1871.

be married in and one can wonder how much material went into the making of this dress.

Anna Swan married Captain Martin Van Buren Bates on June 17, 1871, in London, England. The minister was Reverend Rupert Cochrane, a Nova Scotian Anna had known in her youth. He was well over six feet tall, a large man for that time, but next to the two giants, he looked like a dwarf. Many of the guests were people the giants toured with, such as Christine and Millie, the siamese twins.

The Bates took a short honeymoon trip to Scotland before returning to London to settle into a permanent home. They continued to tour Europe giving receptions for many of the royal families of that time and now appeared together as the "Largest Married Couple in the World". Soon they had to stop touring because Anna was going to have a baby.

On May 19, 1872, Anna gave birth to a gigantic baby girl, weighing about eighteen pounds. The baby died at birth and although Anna and her husband were heartbroken, they allowed the body of the baby to be given to a London hospital for research into the causes of gigantism. When Anna had recovered her health, they went back on tour.

By 1874, Anna and Captain Bates were tired of travelling, of being stared at, and of living in tiny hotel rooms where the beds were too short. Anna had never been completely well since she had lost her baby, and the gigantic couple needed to take some time off from the busy life of show business. They gave up their home in England and sailed for Nova Scotia where Martin finally met Anna's family, friends and neighbours. Nova Scotians had truly missed their "Big

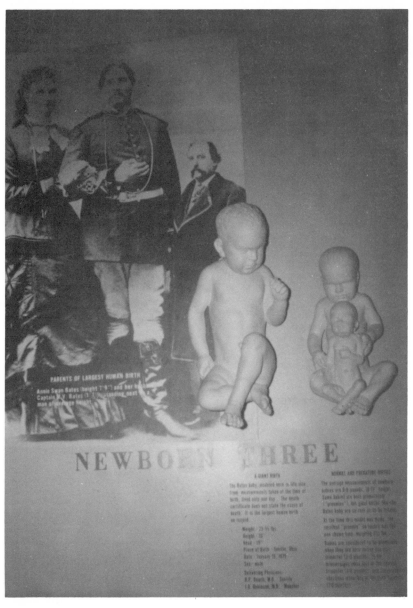

World's largest baby next to other infant models.

Courtesy of G. Swan.

Ann" and were delighted to have her back and to see her so happily married.

The Bates retired from show business and moved to Seville, Ohio, U.S.A. By now they both had plenty of money so they bought a farm and settled down to life in a farming community raising and breeding Percheron horses and Shorthorn cattle.

January 18, 1879, was the day Anna and Martin's second child was born. They were very careful this time and had a doctor waiting to help deliver the baby. A boy was born, weighing over twenty-three pounds, and two and a half feet long. Two doctors did everything they could for him, but the baby lived only eleven hours.

This second tragedy was hard to bear. In 1880 the "Largest Married Couple" made their final tour together. Captain Bates needed more money for his farm and they wanted to build a special house, big enough for two giants. They joined W.W. Cole's Circus, Menagerie, and Museum, touring all over the United States. When they had made enough money, they left show business for ever.

On their farmland, in 1883, the Bates built an enormous house with fourteen large rooms. Martin's shoulders had always been too wide for normal doorways, so he had doors built which he could walk through without turning sideways. The ceilings were fourteen feet high, while the doors were eight and a half feet tall. All the furniture was hand-made to order to fit their two gigantic bodies. At last the colossal couple was comfortable. Martin became a success raising his horses and cattle, and the Bates were loved

Portrait of Anna Swan.

and respected by the people of Seville. Anna became involved in the life of the town, teaching Sunday school at the local church and helping with community projects. Everyone recognized the Bates' special gigantic carriage as it rumbled through town pulled by large Percheron horses.

Annie's health had never been very good and after the deaths of her two babies, she had not recovered the strength of her youth. She was ill for some time after they had built their "dream house". On August 5, 1888, one day away from her forty-second birthday, Anna Swan Bates, the Nova Scotian Giantess, died of "consumption" (a lung ailment). She was buried at Mound Hill Cemetery in Seville, Medina County, Ohio where a life-size statue was placed as a monument over her grave. Her sorrowful parents came from Nova Scotia to mourn their Annie and news of her death was widely reported. From her humble beginnings she had become known and admired the world over and had brought fame to her native province.

From Past to Present

Although these two giants lived and died over one hundred years ago, they are still regarded in Nova Scotia as folk heroes. They were two of the most famous giants ever known and, by touring around the world, they brought fame and honour to their home province.

Angus MacAskill is remembered in the Giant Angus MacAskill Museum in Englishtown, Cape Breton which is run by the Giant Angus MacAskill Heirs Association. Here many of his personal belongings are on display.

A memorial tombstone has been erected over his grave. Many people visit this site which overlooks St. Ann's Bay, to pay their respects to this gentle and good-natured giant.

Anna Swan is buried in Seville, Ohio, and over her grave stands a statue which will help preserve her memory for years to come.

In Tatamagouche, Colchester County, Nova Scotia some of her personal belongings are exhibited at the Fraser Cultural Centre, Sunrise Trail Museum. Here also many photographs of Anna may be seen.

The lives of these two famous giants have often inspired people to write fictional and non-fictional novels, plays and biographies. Sometimes it is hard to separate the facts from the folk tales.

Monument to Anna Swan Bates.

One woman in each of Anna's bloomers!

Courtesy of G. Swan.

One play in particular was a great success. "Giant Anna" by Donna Smyth was written for and performed by Mermaid Theatre of Nova Scotia. Life-sized puppets were used to represent Anna and her husband, Captain Bates. These can be seen at the Fraser Cultural Centre in Tatamagouche.

Today people are used to seeing athletes who might be called giants in sports such as wrestling and basketball. However, if a child grows too much these days, doctors can usually prevent them from becoming abnormally or grotesquely large.

Our two giants overcame what might be regarded as a physical deformity and were able to come to terms with their great size. Nova Scotians recognize their accomplishments and remember them with affection.

Life-sized puppets.

Courtesy of Hilary Sircom.

Bibliography

Almon, Albert. The Nova Scotian Giantess. *New Liberty*, October 11, 1947.

Blakeley, Phyllis R. *Nova Scotia's Two Remarkable Giants*. Lancelot Press Limited, Windsor, Nova Scotia: 1970.

Burrows, Mary. "Anna Swan: Nova Scotia's Famed Giantess." *Chatelaine*, Dec., 1966.

Gillis, James D. *The Cape Breton Giant*. T.C. Allen & Co., Halifax, Nova Scotia: 1926.

Gramly, Allene Holt. *The World's Tallest Couple (The Love Giants)*. Appleseed Press, Mansfield, Ohio: 1981.

Lamb, James B. *The Hidden Heritage*. Lancelot Press Limited, Windsor, Nova Scotia: 1975.

Lotz, Jim & Pat. *Cape Breton Island*. Douglas, David & Charles, Vancouver, British Columbia: 1974.

MacNeil, Neil. *The Highland Heart in Nova Scotia*. Charles Scribner's Sons, New York: 1948.